THE ENDLESS PURSUIT
OF EXCELLENCE

By Robb Thompson

The Endless Pursuit of Excellence
ISBN 1-889723-26-6
Copyright © 2002 by Robb Thompson
Family Harvest Church
18500 92nd Ave.
Tinley Park, Illinois 60477

Editorial Consultant: Cynthia Hansen
Text Design: Lisa Simpson
Cover Design: Greg Lane

TABLE OF CONTENTS

★ ★ ★ ★ ★

CHAPTER ONE

WHAT IS EXCELLENCE?

God is calling us to attention in this day. He's calling us to a deeper life of commitment with Him. Those of us who hear His voice can no longer be willing to live a life of "just good enough." We can never let ourselves be satisfied again with the mediocre and the ordinary, for Heaven's message is clear: A casual attitude toward life will lead us only to a place of disappointment and defeat. If we want to realize God's best for our lives, we must answer His call and launch out on a lifelong pursuit of excellence.

Too often people say they want excellence in their lives but then stop pursuing it because of the cost involved. They become discouraged and quit when they realize it requires a *daily* striving for improvement. They aren't willing to pay the price to obtain the prize.

Excellence is something we have to go after all the time. It is something we must seek for at all times in every way we can. Why? Because the life of God that lives within us demands that we become better tomorrow than we were today.

But what does it mean to be excellent? The truth is, most people can only tell you their *opinion* of what excellence is; they don't really understand what it actually means. So let me give you a idea of all that is encompassed in the word *excellence*.

To achieve excellence means:

- to surpass
- to become better
- to be the best
- to be a champion
- to exceed
- to outdo
- to outshine
- to outstrip
- to transcend

To be excellent is to be:

- high class
- high grade
- exceptional
- premium
- incomparable
- magnificent
- sensational
- superb
- tip top

- famous
- first class
- first rate
- first string
- five star
- front rank
- grade A
- number one
- prime
- royal
- stunning
- superior
- top notch
- unsurpassed

Excellence is meritoriously near the standard, or the model, by which we are all measured. It is imminently good, the best of its kind. Excellence is a noun, not a verb. It is a virtue, a state of being — a part of who a person *is*, not what a person *does*.

Finally, excellence can be obtained. It is measurable. You can see this quality in the life of a person of excellence because he is continually moving in the direction of improvement. He's always getting better. He doesn't take one step forward and three steps backwards.

That person can be *you*, friend. You can make up your mind to go in the direction of betterment all day, every day. As you make a practice of pressing, reaching, and pushing toward excellence, you will also begin to receive the rewards of excellence — every day of your life.

NOTES:

_____

_____

_____

_____

_____

_____

_____

_____

_____

_____

_____

_____

_____

_____

_____

★ ★ ★ ★ ★

STRETCHING FOR THE HIGH ROAD

How well do you measure up in the arena of excellence?

That isn't a question any of us can answer once and for all, for we're all growing. Excellence is a living word that continues to reach, to move on, to press forward. No matter what level of excellence we have reached to this moment, there is always another level, a higher road. We can always become better tomorrow, for none of us has ever yet "arrived."

Ever since I was first saved, I've never stopped "stretching for the higher road" in my own walk with God. Back then I wasn't thinking about entering the ministry. I never thought that I would one day be someone whom people around the world would recognize and know. I never set out to reach that goal, and even now I am not seeking to be known.

So how did my life turn out the way it has? There is only one reason: *All I have ever desired to do is pursue Jesus with all my heart and please Him to the best of my understanding at every moment.*

That's why the pursuit of excellence is always on my mind. I live with the thought pattern of always getting better, always multiplying, always becoming more effective. I wake up every morning with the question, *What can I do today to reach beyond where I am right now?*

This is not an easy road for any of us to take. Therefore, I'd like to offer some suggestions in this book and possibly answer any questions you might have regarding the pursuit of excellence.

What can we do each day to press forward to a higher level of excellence in every area of our lives — our marriages, our families, our jobs, our churches, and our relationships? Here are some principles of excellence that we can follow to help us do just that.

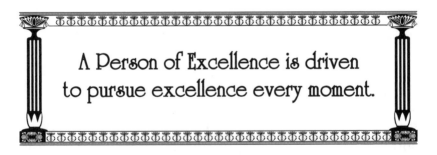

A Person of Excellence is driven to pursue excellence every moment.

The first thing we have to understand is that we will never attain perfection in this life because two things didn't get saved when we got saved: 1) our minds, and 2) our bodies. Those two parts of us will continually try to drag us back down to the earth and keep us out of the heavenlies. Nevertheless, it is still our job to pursue excellence every moment of every day.

You see, God promises us a wonderful future in Jeremiah 29:11:

"For I know the thoughts that I think toward you, says the Lord, thoughts of peace and not of evil, to give you a future and a hope."

But notice the two verses that come next are an essential part of that promise:

"Then you will call upon Me and go and pray to Me, and I will listen to you.
"And you will seek Me and find Me, when you search for Me with all your heart."

Jeremiah 29:12,13

We must *press in* to realize God's best for our lives. Just as Paul did in Philippians 3:13, we must place our focus on **"...forgetting those things which are behind and reaching forward to those things which are ahead."**

So when you wake up in the morning, immediately center your thoughts on how you can move one step closer to your destination of excellence than you were yesterday. Every day take a step forward; then drive a stake in the ground where you stand and declare, "I will never go back any further than where I am right now!"

I know it isn't always easy to do that. But once you make a move to become better in a certain area of your life, you have to hold on to what you've accomplished. Even if you run into a storm, just keep holding on and *refuse* to take a step backwards.

You see, if we run away from a storm when it arises, we'll just have to face it again later — and the next time we face the storm, it will be even more difficult to overcome. Why is this? *Because our enemy is at his weakest point the day we meet him.* If we try to brush him away and put him off for the future, he'll just come back at a time when we can't handle him.

So as soon as you see something in your flesh that needs to change, don't ignore it. Lock in on it immediately and deal with it. Don't be afraid of the enemy, for the moment you become a grasshopper in your own sight is the moment your enemy wins.

In Numbers 13:31-33, we see that ten of the twelve men Moses sent to spy out the Promised Land made that very mistake:

> **But the men who had gone up with him** [Caleb] **said, "We are not able to go up against the people, for they are stronger than we."**
> **And they gave the children of Israel a bad report of the land which they had spied out, saying, "The land through which we have gone as spies is a land that devours its inhabitants, and all the people whom we saw in it are men of great stature.**

"There we saw the giants (the descendants of Anak came from the giants); and we were like grasshoppers in our own sight, and so we were in their sight."

Those ten spies paid the consequences for that evil report, for they were never allowed to enter the Promised Land again.

Thank God, that never has to be *your* story. The Word says that God has made you more than a conqueror in Christ (Rom. 8:37). That means you don't have to let *anything* hinder you for even a moment from your daily pursuit of personal excellence!

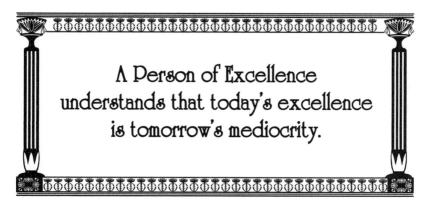

A Person of Excellence understands that today's excellence is tomorrow's mediocrity.

Tomorrow my level of excellence will be greater than my level of excellence today. I'll say it another way: What I expect out of my life today is less than what I will expect out of my life tomorrow. That's why I'm always thinking, *What can I do better tomorrow? How can I improve in this relationship, in this area of my life, in my job performance?*

We must always keep in mind that excellence is like the manna God sent to the children of Israel in the wilderness. One level of excellence only lasts for a little while before it becomes stale mediocrity. That's why we can never stop moving up to the next level of excellence in our walk with God.

We have to make the decision, "My excellence of today is as far back as I'm going to go for my tomorrow. I will never go back any further than the level of excellence I have attained today."

Remember, friend, excellence is not a destination; it's a journey. It is not an event; it is a process. You don't instantaneously achieve excellence by making the decision to be excellent. You don't become excellent by attending one more seminar.

Excellence is something we go *through* every day, not something we go *to* every day. It's something that lives on the inside of us, continually drawing us forward to becoming better than we were yesterday until we transcend even the highest levels of expectation.

Excellence comes in time, without fanfare, almost without being noticed. It begins to gradually show up in our lives as we continue to press toward the mark of becoming whatever God desires for us in every area of our lives. Then one day without even being aware of it, we step into a new realm where excellence is the standard and mediocrity is not tolerated.

But it all begins with a disciplined lifestyle that transforms into a system by which we live our lives. We set our lives in a direction that conforms to God's requirements in the Word. Then we refuse to change that direction leading to excellence regardless of any circumstances that may arise to distract us.

The truth is, the content of the message you're writing for your life twenty years from now is determined by either the mediocrity or the excellence by which you are living your life today. That's how important it is to choose excellence over mediocrity in every situation of life.

However, excellence may be something completely different to you than it is to another person because God always uses the measuring stick of your own potential to determine your level of excellence. You see, it doesn't matter *what type* of potential you have; it matters *how much* of your potential you are pursuing and using.

But although excellence may mean two different things to two different people who are diligently pursuing that high goal, the end result will be the same for both of them: They will both one day stand in a place of honor before great people. How do I know that? Proverbs 22:29 tells me so!

Do you see a man who excels in his work? He will stand before kings; he will not stand before unknown men.

> A Person of Excellence realizes
> that he has never arrived,
> so he just continues
> on his journey.

I've had people say to me, "Oh, I just love to do anything I can for you."

I may respond with something as simple as "Thank you. That is very kind."

Then as the person turns to go, an overwhelming sense of love sometimes comes over me, and I seem to know why he or she is having such a hard time in life. So I turn to the person and ask, "Do you remember the last time you said those words to me about six months ago? Did you ever take care of what I asked you to do then?"

"No, I didn't, but I'd just do anything for you, Pastor Robb."

"Well, why don't you do what you said you'd do six months ago? Then we'll go from there."

This is the kind of conversation a person of excellence never has with those to whom he is assigned. He doesn't ask, "How can I do more for you today?" when he hasn't taken care of the task he was asked to do yesterday. Meanwhile, he just keeps pushing himself to ensure that the next performance of his responsibilities is always better than the last one.

That's why we must always stay in a learning mode as people of excellence. We must never stop sharpening our skills, our abilities, our character. Our lifelong attitude should be "I can become more. I can do more. I don't have to stay the same."

If I try to change everything that needs to change in my life all at once, I won't be able to sustain the pain of that change. But I know I can become the best God has made me to be if I will only take my pursuit of excellence one step and one day at a time.

However, just because I'm a person of excellence doesn't mean I'm a perfectionist. No, I've made peace with myself. I know that no matter how much I kick myself, I'm still going to be the same person *after* I kick myself as I was *before*. So I accept myself right where I am right now. I am who I am — but at the same time, nothing is going to stop me from becoming better! Even though I accept myself the way I am, I know I don't have to stay that way.

That's the difference between a perfectionist and a person of excellence. A perfectionist is never really happy because he never reaches his goal of perfection. But a person of excellence is always happy because he knows he's headed in the right direction. He may not have arrived at his destination yet, but, thank God, he's on his way!

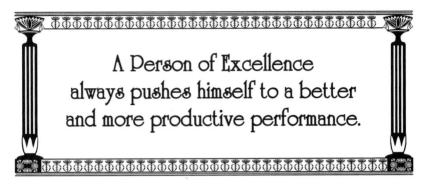

A Person of Excellence always pushes himself to a better and more productive performance.

The excellent continually push themselves to perform twenty-four hours a day, seven days a week. On the other hand, those who are content to stay common and ordinary only enjoy moments of greatness.

The common visit excellence for moments, but in their minds, they think they are doing great all the time. They're always thinking about the nice thing they did last week or last month. Yet they wonder why they wait year after year for someone to recognize their achievements and promote them. They don't realize that their pride and their refusal to be corrected have made them unapproachable for promotion. This is a very sad but common scenario.

We can never be promoted in life without correction, friend, because none of us are perfect. Every one of us has imperfections that we have to face. However, as long as we continue to pursue excellence, we will always be headed in the direction that will ultimately make us more like Jesus, the Lord of all.

Personally, I want to stay approachable so I can be corrected when I need to be. I don't want to sit around thinking I have my act together when I don't. I don't want it written on my gravestone one day, "He *thought* he had it all together." That's why I push to perform better than I did yesterday every day of my life.

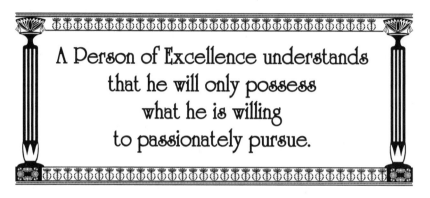

A Person of Excellence understands
that he will only possess
what he is willing
to passionately pursue.

The proof of desire is pursuit. You see, excellence is a reality to live in every moment of every day. It isn't something we camp out at for a while. It is something we have to continually seek after and pursue.

Whatever we lack in life, we can trace the reason for that lack to one thing: We've been unwilling to give our time to the pursuit of that goal. We'll never obtain what we're unwilling to invest our time to obtain. If we truly desire something, we'll pursue it. If we don't go after it, it is safe to say we really don't want it.

So many people say they want to be excellent, yet they don't pursue it. Instead, they live their lives in mediocrity with a "just good enough" attitude. Year after year, it's always the same; they stay right in the middle of the pack because they don't want excellence enough to trade their time for it.

But when we start moving in the direction of excellence, we no longer compete with others; we now start competing with *ourselves*. And if we will keep moving in that direction, we will eventually transcend the highest level of the expectations that others place on us. Excellence will come alive in our lives — not just for a moment in time, but for a lifetime.

Jean-Claude Killy is a good example of this principle. Killy is a French alpine skier who won three gold medals at the 1968 Olympic games in Grenoble, France. He won the downhill race event by a mere three-tenths of a second. Yet in the year following that race, Jean-Claude earned three million dollars, and everyone still knows who he is. In fact, many credit him with being the greatest downhill skier of all time.

On the other hand, very few people can tell you who came in second in that downhill race. The second-place skier was just three-tenths of a second behind Jean-Claude, but in the same year that Killy made three million dollars as a result of winning the gold medal, the skier who came in second made only $30,000 as a ski instructor.

Jean-Claude Killy won that year because he was a man who pursued personal excellence. He wasn't racing against another person; he was racing against himself. He had the attitude, *It isn't enough to beat everyone else. I have to beat myself. Whatever mediocrity I conquered in the trials of life yesterday, I must transcend today.*

That's also how I keep myself on the road to excellence. I don't compare myself to others. I just keep trying to beat my own best time in the spiritual race set before me!

Most people are very uncomfortable with that mentality. They can't take the pressure of continually progressing forward. But while they're stuck in a rut of mediocrity, the person of excellence continues to conquer more obstacles and achieve higher goals each day. Why? Because he is determined to become all God has called him to become!

This isn't a *message* I'm sharing with you; it's a *lifestyle*. And when you begin to understand how to live this lifestyle, it will change your socioeconomic background forever.

You see, where we are today is where our parents brought us, but the Word will take us where our Father God is calling us to go in life — to a higher level, to a new way of living. However, we are the ones who have to decide which parent we are going to identify with. It's *our* choice.

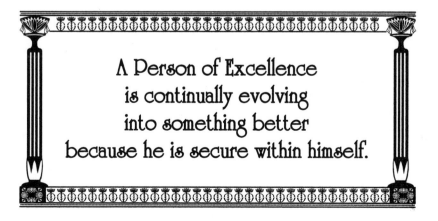

A Person of Excellence
is continually evolving
into something better
because he is secure within himself.

A person of excellence never has to have anyone talk to him about his performance. He's risen above that level of correction because he is already motivated by his own inner drive to become better. That's why he has long since left the shore of competing with someone else and is instead always competing against himself.

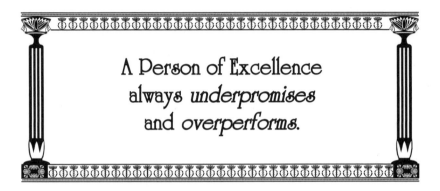

A Person of Excellence
always *underpromises*
and *overperforms*.

No one ever has to talk to me about doing more; I'm going to do more before someone who is over me ever opens his mouth. I'm always looking for what I can do today that surpasses anything I might have done yesterday.

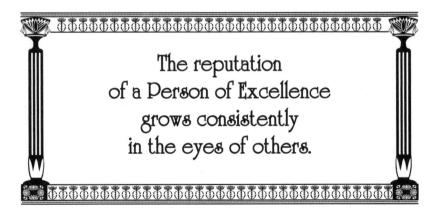

The reputation
of a Person of Excellence
grows consistently
in the eyes of others.

The more people get to know us, the more impressed they should be with us. That must be our goal in all our relationships.

Too often the opposite is true. When you first meet a person, you think he's wonderful. But after you've known that person for a while, you begin to see that he isn't as wonderful as you first thought he was!

It isn't that way with God. James 1:17 (*KJV*) says, **"Every good gift and every perfect gift is from above, and cometh down from the Father of lights, with whom is no variableness, neither shadow of turning."** This scripture gives us the understanding that even if we get right up close to God, we won't see anything different in His nature than what the Word presents Him to be. The closer we get to God, the more assured we are that He will not fail to give us good and perfect gifts. The closer we get to Him, the better He looks — and so it should be with us.

We must grow in our reputation in the eyes of others and continually exceed their expectations. Every time they see us, they should like us more and be even more convinced of our excellence.

This principle is certainly true in the business realm. You have to build a reputation, whether you're an insurance salesman, a real estate broker, or an airline pilot. If you're in the insurance business, you have to build up a clientele so you can have the residuals to make some money. If you own a gas station, you have to make sure people know where your station is. It takes awhile for customers to start figuring out that they need to stop and get their car serviced right where you are.

Building a reputation takes time. It also requires diligence as we press forward into excellence.

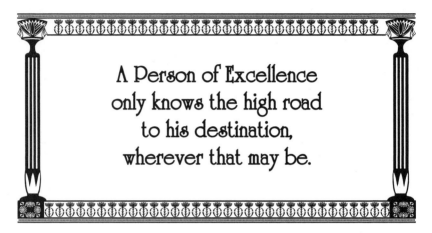

A Person of Excellence only knows the high road to his destination, wherever that may be.

I am determined to always take the high road — the road God takes — in every situation. I'm going to keep on pressing toward the mark for the prize of the high calling of God (Phil. 3:14).

There once lived a Roman philosopher named Epictetus who lived from 55 AD to 135 AD. I remember reading something Epictetus wrote that I consider very interesting. In essence, this is what the philosopher said: *You must decide to construct your character through excellent actions and determine to pay the price of a worthy goal. The trials you encounter will introduce you to your strengths.*

I can rest assured that in my pursuit of excellence, I will experience some trials along the way.

However, those trials can serve to take me closer to my goal if I allow them to introduce me to the strength I have in Christ through faith in His Word.

At times circumstances will tell me, "You don't want to do this. This is going to be too much, too hard. Why do you have to set your standards so high?"

But my standards aren't too high. How can I tell God that I love Him and then turn right around and say, "Lord, it would be nice if You put the bar down a couple notches"?

No, I just say, "God, I don't set the standard for me to live by; You do. So You put the bar wherever You want to put it. I may spend most of my life trying to clear the bar without falling, but at least I'm going for it. I'm stretching myself for the high road You want me to take, not the low road my flesh wants to take!"

PRINCIPLES FOR
THE PURSUIT OF EXCELLENCE

⋆ **A Person of Excellence is driven to pursue excellence every moment.**

⋆ **A Person of Excellence understands that today's excellence is tomorrow's mediocrity.**

⋆ **A Person of Excellence realizes that he has never arrived, so he just continues on his journey.**

⋆ **A Person of Excellence always pushes himself to a better and more productive performance.**

* A Person of Excellence understands that he will only possess what he is willing to passionately pursue.

* A Person of Excellence is continually evolving into something better because he is secure within himself.

* A Person of Excellence always *underpromises* and *overperforms*.

* The reputation of a Person of Excellence grows consistently in the eyes of others.

* A Person of Excellence only knows the high road to his destination, wherever that may be.

NOTES:

_____

_____

_____

_____

_____

_____

_____

_____

_____

★ ★ ★ ★ ★

NO SHORTCUTS TO EXCELLENCE

Many people want to take a shortcut on the road to excellence. These are often the people who end up rebelling or walking away from the commitments in life they have made as well as away from the church.

John 6 tells us that Jesus ran into this same problem. The people who were following Jesus were all excited about His ministry. They asked Him, "What must we do to work the works of God?" (John 6:28).

Among other things, Jesus said this in reply:

"Whoever eats My flesh and drinks My blood has eternal life, and I will raise him up at the last day."

John 6:54

The Jews didn't know what to do with Jesus' unusual words. Verse 66 relates what happened next:

From that time many of His disciples went back and walked with Him no more.

So Jesus turned to His twelve disciples and asked, "Are you guys going to leave too?"

Peter piped up and said in effect, "There is no other church that would accept our mediocrity, Jesus. Where would we go?"

But Jesus had just given His disciples the answer they needed, if they would only receive it:

"It is the Spirit who gives life; the flesh profits nothing. The words that I speak to you are spirit, and they are life."

John 6:63

With these words, Jesus let His disciples know that if they'd continue to abide in Him, His words of spirit and life would work in their lives and eventually make them what God wanted them to be.

You see, when God's Word begins to work on the inside of us, it takes time for that Word to be manifested on the outside. Just as a baby doesn't come forth from the mother's womb until he is ready, so God's Word only comes forth from us in due time.

You may ask, "But are there any shortcuts I can take after I've planted the seed of the Word to make my 'due time' come faster?" Let me share some more principles of excellence to help answer that question.

The Pharmacy America Trusts

I'm VERONICA. I'm here to serve you
with our "7 Service Basics"

247   10   4414   05713   028

RFN# 0571-3284-4145-0308-1020

B/DM ALMD 6Z	1B	2.99	
S/F BAR 8PK	1B	5.79	
N/VLY BAR12Z	B	2.69	SALE
SUBTOTAL		11.47	

B=2% SALES TAX	.23
TOTAL	11.70

CASH	20.00
CHANGE	8.30

WAG ADVERTISED SAVINGS: .30

YOUR TOTAL SAVINGS: .30

![Walgreens logo]

Items purchased at Walgreens may be
returned to any of our stores within
30 days of purchase.

Items with a receipt will be exchanged,
refunded in cash or credited to your account.

Items without a receipt will be exchanged or
refunded by mail within 14 days.

For any return you may be asked for
acceptable identification.

![Walgreens logo]

Items purchased at Walgreens may be
returned to any of our stores within
30 days of purchase.

Items with a receipt will be exchanged,
refunded in cash or credited to your account.

Items without a receipt will be exchanged or
refunded by mail within 14 days.

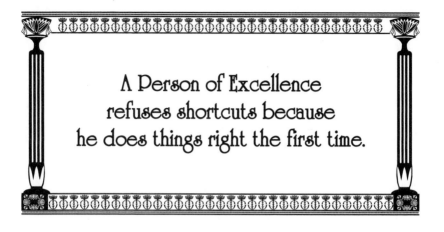

Λ Person of Excellence
refuses shortcuts because
he does things right the first time.

We may as well stop looking for a shortcut to excellence in our lives, because there is no such thing. If we are truly going to pursue excellence, we have to refuse to put things off that we need to do and work on getting ourselves into a routine.

Our success in life is actually linked to our routines. If we don't get into the routine of paying our bills on time, we'll always pay them late. If we don't choose to put our clothes away every day, our clothes will become a part of the permanent clutter in our homes. If we don't understand that every dime coming through our hands has a specific assignment and is not necessarily ours to spend as we like, we will never increase.

That's why we must work on developing the routines of a disciplined lifestyle. Although there are no shortcuts to excellence, we *can* make sure we don't unnecessarily prolong our journey along the way!

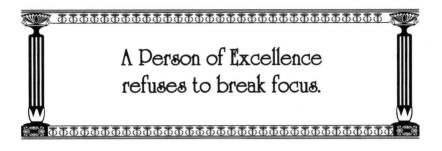

A Person of Excellence
refuses to break focus.

Proverbs 29:18 (*KJV*) says, **"Where there is no vision, the people perish...."** This is the reason people of excellence refuse to break focus. They realize that the consequences of doing so would involve perishing in many areas of their lives.

The mediocre always focus on what they're *going through*. In order to be effective in our pursuit of excellence, we must choose to focus on what we're *going to*. In other words, we have to focus our decisions, our desires, and our direction like invisible laser beams centered on a single point in the distance — the fulfillment of God's purpose for our lives.

The truth is, one of our greatest enemies in life is *broken focus*. For instance, suppose one day you decide you're going to start getting up early in the morning to pray. So you get up and decide to make yourself a cup of coffee first. All of a sudden, you hear one of your kids yelling for you to come help him with something. You run to take care of that situation, thinking, *Jesus, I'm coming. I'll be there in a minute.* Then the phone rings, and that conversation takes another fifteen minutes. Soon the morning is half gone, and you have to leave for a scheduled appointment.

This type of situation happens again and again to Christians in many arenas of life. A day turns into a week; a week turns into a month; and a month turns into a year. All of a sudden, people look back at their lives and think, *What a fool I've been! I concentrated on things I never should have bothered with — all because of broken focus.*

Fear is one of the most effective tools the devil uses to break our focus. You see, fear is a master. When we allow ourselves to be driven by fear, it tries to force us to submit to it, making us listen to thoughts of worry and anxiety all day long.

But we don't have to submit to fear. We have a choice in the matter: What are we going to focus on — what we're going *through*, or what we're going *to*?

Finances are another great challenge to our focus on excellence. In fact, finances can be our greatest test. As we begin to accumulate wealth in our lives, it's easy to start feeling like we don't need God as much as we used to.

In fact, that's one of the reasons the Gospel is so accepted in very poor countries. The people who live in these countries often have nothing. The only One who can help them is God.

But God wants us to choose Him freely — not just because our backs are against the wall and we have the devil's hand on our throats. He wants us to prosper in every area of our lives as we continue to focus on Him.

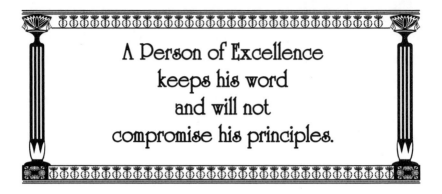

A Person of Excellence
keeps his word
and will not
compromise his principles.

Proverbs 4:7 says, **"Wisdom is the principal thing...."** But let me tell you something even greater: Wisdom is also the *principled* thing! If you are a person of excellence who never veers off the path of the godly principles you've established in your life, the Bible calls you *wise*.

Ever since the 1970s, modern society has promoted situational ethics as the new reality. Ethics change depending on which side of the table a person happens to be sitting on. This is the hallmark of the religious, by the way. The double standard is always the accepted practice.

But a double standard is *never* an accepted practice with God. Proverbs 11:1 (*KJV*) says, **"A false balance is abomination to the Lord: but a just weight is his delight."** That's why God's principles must be the bedrock foundation of our lives.

You know, the foundation of a house is something people often forget to consider when they buy a home. But the truth is, nothing is more important than the foundation, both in the natural and in the spiritual realm.

A few years ago, I traveled to California with Peter Daniels to meet with Robert Schuller. During our visit, Bob mentioned to me that when people move to California, they look at the sky and say it's beautiful. They feel the climate and say it's wonderful. But the one thing they never think about is the ground under their feet. Some have even bought property on top of the San Andreas fault! Those people don't realize that the foundation is the most important consideration of all when building a home.

Jesus built a solid foundation in His own life for thirty years before beginning His ministry — a ministry that lasted only three and a half years. During those years of ministry, Jesus' focus continued to be on building a foundation — this time in the lives of the people who would receive His sayings.

Often when Jesus talked to people about their lives, He'd speak to them concerning their foundation. Luke 6:46-50 is the classic example:

"But why do you call Me 'Lord, Lord,' and do not do the things which I say?
"Whoever comes to Me, and hears My sayings and does them, I will show you whom he is like:
"He is like a man building a house, who dug deep and laid the foundation on the rock. And when the flood arose, the stream beat vehemently against that house, and

could not shake it, for it was founded on the rock.

"But he who heard and did nothing is like a man who built a house on the earth without a foundation, against which the stream beat vehemently; and immediately it fell. And the ruin of that house was great."

As for me, my determined purpose has always been to build the foundation of my life on the principles of God's Word. My principles don't change just because the situations or the relationships in my life change. No matter what, I certainly never intend to compromise, nor from my perspective *do* I compromise, the scriptural foundation I've already established.

Over the years, I've come to recognize one of the greatest travesties in America today: *Too often people prize relationship over integrity.* A person can never do that if he wants to stay on track in the pursuit of excellence.

One of the misconceptions people sometimes have about me is that I tend to discard people with whom I've had relationship. Although I've never discarded a relationship, it is true that a person may disqualify himself by attempting to go backwards in his relationship with me. In other words, he may want to enjoy the intimacy of a "level four" relationship with me while at the same time regressing in his lifestyle to the lower principles of a "level two" relationship.

I can't do that. I will not prize that relationship above the integrity it reached at its highest level. That person may come to me and ask, "What changed between us?" Well, something may have changed, but it wasn't me. I'm still living according to the highest level we achieved in our relationship.

He may protest, "But I thought you were my friend!" But Proverbs 27:6 says, **"Faithful are the wounds of a friend, but the kisses of an enemy are deceitful."** The problem is, too many Christians are "kissing" each other all the time — making excuses for compromise and sin — when they need to be "wounding" each other by speaking the truth in love!

At times you may think that in order to keep your friends, you have to compromise. But if someone causes you to compromise your principles, he isn't your friend anyway.

In order to be a person of principle, you have to refuse to allow any person or circumstance to cause you to compromise what you believe is right. That way no matter what situation comes up, you'll know the direction you should take in making decisions.

I never compromise my principles for anyone, anywhere in the world — ever! Do you know why? Because I have to go home with me. You see, the moment I decide to compromise, I've placed myself on another playing field where I have to believe in the word of someone else in order for me to experience success in my own life.

Let me give you a case in point. Proverbs 6:2 (*TLB*) talks about the folly of cosigning a loan for someone:

Son, if you endorse a note for someone you hardly know, guaranteeing his debt, you are in serious trouble.

You may have trapped yourself by your agreement.

Quick! Get out of it if you possibly can! Swallow your pride; don't let embarrassment stand in the way. Go and beg to have your name erased.

If you identify with this passage of Scripture — if you've ever cosigned a loan for someone else and wished you hadn't done that — here's why: There's always a reason why a person needs a cosigner in order to secure a loan to purchase something. That is God's cue telling him it isn't time for him to obtain the material possession he's pursuing. God is telling that person, "Not now. Later on you'll be able to get that — when you can believe for it yourself."

The person who has asked you to help him secure a loan doesn't need you — he needs to believe *God* for his needs to be met. If you cosign for him, the Bible says you will be snared.

So don't start compromising your principles to please people, for those people will only cause you to spiral downward as they use you to lend credibility to their unfaithfulness. Just stay focused on obeying the Word and pursuing excellence in your life. Live as a principled person, and you will always be pleasing to God!

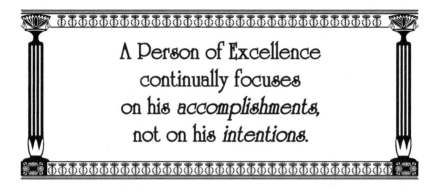

A Person of Excellence
continually focuses
on his accomplishments,
not on his *intentions.*

The common man lives in a dream world of intentions. He thinks in his mind that he's doing something when in fact he has accomplished nothing at all. Therefore, he's continually saying, "Oh, I didn't mean to do that"; "I really intended to get that assignment finished by today, but I wasn't able to get to it"; or "I don't know what happened. I really meant to do it right, but it just didn't come out right."

The problem is, a person isn't rewarded for his intentions; he is rewarded for his *accomplishments.* Thus, if he lives his life by intentions, he is destined to go nowhere.

Interestingly, people who judge themselves by their *intentions* most often judge others by their *actions.* They need to use the same litmus test on themselves and examine their own track record!

The question that continually needs to be on my mind is this: *Did I accomplish that goal? Did I finish what I set out to do?* I don't need to be thinking, *This is just too hard! I can't do it. Isn't it enough that I really did intend to accomplish this goal, even if I give up and quit?*

God never asked us to do one easy thing yet. That's why He calls it a walk of faith! The day you think God has asked you to do something easy is the day you can know it wasn't God.

How do I know that? Because whatever God asks you to do, He wants you to do it by faith. He will never give you something to do that you can accomplish in your own ability because He never provides shortcuts on the road to excellence.

So how badly do you want excellence in your life, friend? Are you willing to do what it takes to achieve it? If your answer is yes, then step up to the starting line, and get ready for a race that has no end in this life. Regardless of the cost, pursue excellence without compromise, and move upward, ever upward, to a higher road!

PRINCIPLES FOR
REFUSING SHORTCUTS TO EXCELLENCE

⋆ **A Person of Excellence refuses shortcuts because he does things right the first time.**

⋆ **A Person of Excellence refuses to break focus.**

⋆ **A Person of Excellence keeps his word and will not compromise his principles.**

⋆ **A Person of Excellence continually focuses on his *accomplishments*, not on his *intentions*.**

Notes:

_____

_____

_____

_____

_____

_____

_____

_____

_____

_____

_____

_____

_____

_____

_____

_____

_____

_____

_____

_____

_____

PRAYER OF SALVATION

Perhaps you have never been born again and therefore haven't even begun the pursuit of excellence in God. If you have never received Jesus Christ as your personal Lord and Savior and would like to do that right now, just pray this simple prayer:

Dear Lord Jesus, I know that I am lost and need Your forgiveness. I believe that You died for me on the Cross and that God raised You from the dead. I now invite You to come into my heart to be my Lord and Savior. Forgive me of all sin in my life and make me who You want me to be. Amen.

If you prayed this prayer from your heart, congratulations! You have just changed your destiny and will spend eternity with God. Your sins were forgiven the moment you made Jesus the Lord of your life. Now God sees you as pure and holy, as if you had never sinned. You have been set free from the bondage of sin!

OTHER BOOKS
BY ROBB THOMPSON

Victory Over Fear

The Winning Decision

You Are Healed

Marriage From God's Perspective

*The Great Exchange:
Your Thoughts for God's Thoughts*

Winning the Heart of God

Shattered Dreams

Excellence in Ministry

Excellence in the Workplace

Excellence in Attitude

For a complete listing
of additional products
by Robb Thompson, please call:

**1-877-WIN-LIFE
(1-877-946-5433)**

You can also visit us on the web at:
www.winninginlife.org

To contact Robb Thompson,
please write:

Robb Thompson
P. O. Box 558009
Chicago, Illinois 60655

Please include your prayer requests
and comments when you write.

ABOUT THE AUTHOR

For almost two decades, Robb Thompson has pastored the congregation of Family Harvest Church in Tinley Park, Illinois, reaching out to the Chicago area with a practical, easily understood message of "Walking in Excellence." A hallmark of his exciting ministry has been his ability to teach Christians how to act on God's Word and move out in faith so they can become people of excellence and winners in this life. Today, Robb Thompson's teaching ministry continues to grow through books, tapes, and the ever-expanding television program, *Winning in Life,* as he ministers to people throughout the United States and around the world.